Colour in Hope

Text compiled by Becki Bradshaw
Illustrations copyright © 2017 James Newman Gray
This edition copyright © 2017 Lion Hudson

Published by Lion Books
an imprint of
Lion Hudson plc
Wilkinson House, Jordan Hill Road,
Oxford OX2 8DR, England
www.lionhudson.com/lion

ISBN 978 0 7459 8005 8

First edition 2017

Acknowledgments
Scripture quotations taken from the Holy Bible, New International
Version Anglicised. Copyright © 1979, 1984, 2011 Biblica, formerly
International Bible Society. Used by permission of Hodder &
Stoughton Ltd, an Hachette UK company. All rights reserved. "NIV" is
a registered trademark of Biblica. UK trademark number 1448790.

A catalogue record for this book is available from the British Library

Printed and bound in Poland, January 2017, LH52

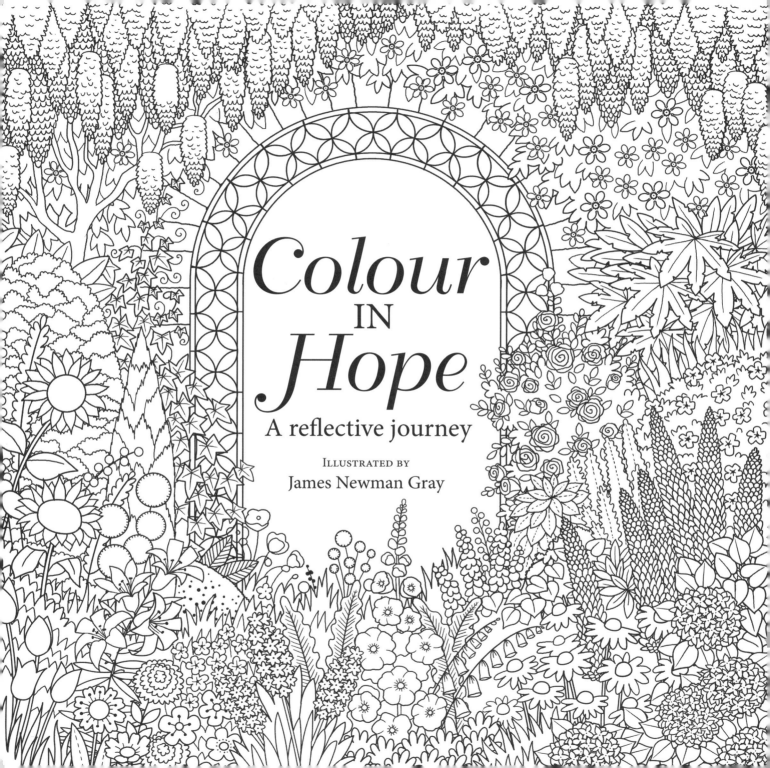

Colour
IN
Hope

A reflective journey

ILLUSTRATED BY
James Newman Gray

*Hope is like the sun, which, as we journey toward it,
casts the shadow of our burden behind us.*

Samuel Smiles

Hope is patience with the lamp lit.

Tertullian

Hope
Smiles from the threshold of the year to come
Whispering "It will be happier"…

Alfred Tennyson

*We must accept finite disappointment, but we must
never lose infinite hope.*

Martin Luther King Jr.

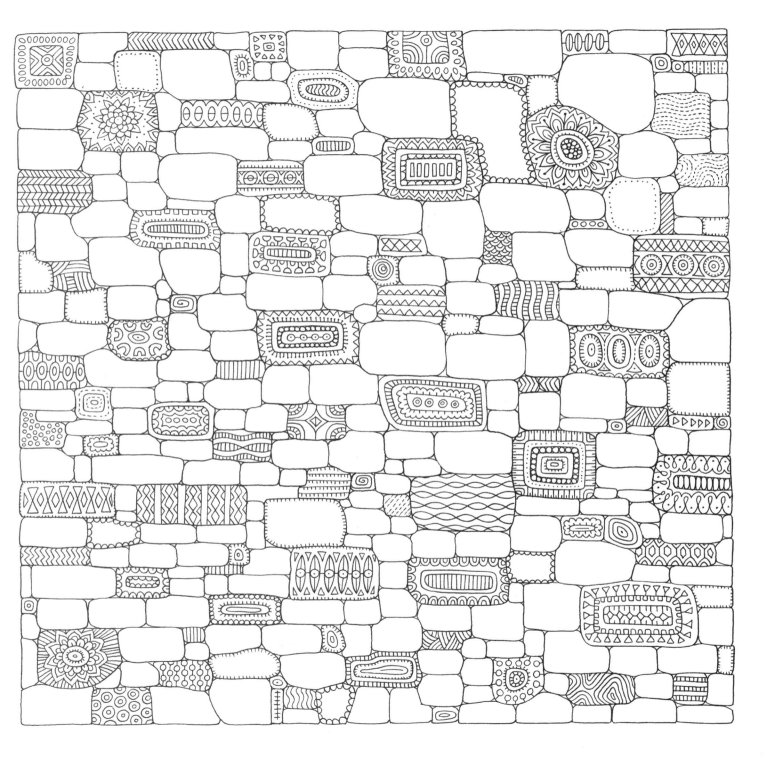

Be joyful in hope, patient in affliction,
faithful in prayer.

Romans 12:12

Hope is the pillar that holds up the world.
Hope is the dream of a waking man.

Pliny the Elder

… but those who hope in the Lord
will renew their strength.
They will soar on wings like eagles;
they will run and not grow weary,
they will walk and not be faint.

Isaiah 40:31

Use these pages for your own doodles, thoughts, and scribbles…